Trombone

IMMORTAL
FOLKSONGS

arranged for brass
by Terry Vosbe[in]

easy level

THE CANADIAN
BRASS

CANADIAN
BRASS
SERIES OF
COLLECTED QUINTETS

SIMPLE GIFTS

TROMBONE

Traditional
arranged by Terry Vosbein

SHENANDOAH

TROMBONE

Traditional
arranged by Terry Vosbein

Londonderry Air

TROMBONE

Traditional
arranged by Terry Vosbein

Tranquillo (♩ = 60)

rit.

HIGH BARBARY

TROMBONE

Traditional
arranged by Terry Vosbein

GREENSLEEVES

TROMBONE

Traditional
arranged by Terry Vosbein

THE DRUNKEN SAILOR

TROMBONE

Traditional
arranged by Terry Vosbein

CANADIAN BRASS

SERIES OF COLLECTED QUINTETS

IMMORTAL FOLKSONGS

arranged for brass quintet
by Terry Vosbein

contents

Welcome to the Canadian Brass Series of Collected Quintets. In our work with students, for some time we have been aware of the need for more brass quintet music at easy and intermediate levels of difficulty. We are continually observing a kind of "Renaissance" in brass music, not only in audience responses to our quintet, but to all brass music in general. The brass quintet, as a chamber ensemble, seems to have become as standard a chamber combination as a string quartet. That could not have been said twenty-five years ago. Brass quintets are popping up everywhere — professional quintets, junior and senior high school ensembles, college and university groups, and amateur quintets of adult players.

We have carefully chosen the literature for these collected quintets, and closely supervised the arrangements. Our aim was to retain a Canadian Brass flavor to each arrangement, and create attractive repertory designed so that any brass quintet can play it with satisfying results. We've often remarked to one another that we certainly wish that we'd had quintet arrangements like these when we were students!

Happy playing to you and your quintet.

— THE CANADIAN BRASS

U.S. $8.99

ISBN-13: 978-1-4584-0181-6
Distributed By
HAL LEONARD
50488775   9 781458 401816

HAL•LEONARD® CORPORATION
7777 W. BLUEMOUND RD. P.O. BOX 13819 MILWAUKEE, WI 53213

0 73999 88775 4
HL50488775